DO YOU HAVE A LOVED ONE IN JAIL?

DR. MARVIN SCOTT, Ph.D.

Xulon PRESS

Copyright © 2004 by Dr. Marvin Scott

Do You Have A Loved One In Jail?
by Dr. Marvin Scott

Printed in the United States of America

ISBN 1-594677-42-5

All rights reserved solely by the author. The author guarantees all contents are original and do not infringe upon the legal rights of any other person or work. This book is protected under the copyright laws of the United States of America. This book may not be copied or reprinted for any use. The views expressed in this book are not necessarily those of the publisher.

Unless otherwise indicated, Bible quotations are taken from NIV version of the Bible. Copyright © 1985 by The Zondervan Corporation.

www.xulonpress.com

Contents

Dedication vii

Acknowledgments ix

Introduction xi

Chapter 1   Know This 15

Chapter 2   Victims of Circumstance 29

Chapter 3   Forgiveness 35

Chapter 4   Sick and Tired of Being Sick and Tired 53

Chapter 5	Are You Under a Load?............61
Chapter 6	Pressured to Perform 71
Chapter 7	The Silent Frustration of Masturbation..............................79
Chapter 8	Turning Your Experience Into Ministry 95
Chapter 9	Free at Last 107

Conclusion..

Summary ....

Dedication

I dedicate this book to those who are praying but still find themselves worried about their loved ones who are in jail. I also dedicate this book to inmates who are tired of repeating the cycle time and time again. May the yoke of bondage be broken once and for all.

Acknowledgments

Special Thanks to God; who inspires and enables me with the ability to do the things I do in His kingdom.

My wife, who believes in me and for praying for me while I spend many hours away from home ministering behind bars.

My church family, Outreach Deliverance Center, Alexandria, Virginia. Thanks for your prayers and support.

The inmates I have met over the past six years in bible class. You have provided me with a wealth of knowledge by interacting with me in class or in a one-on-one counseling session.

Ms. Vickie Williams for your editorial support and prayers. Special thanks for going that extra mile.

Introduction

Each month an alarming number of former inmates return to jail because they cannot manage their lives. It is my goal to see this number decrease. I want to educate those that I come in contact with, whether behind bars or on the streets, because being locked-up is not solving the problems that our men and women are facing.

I have been involved in prison ministry for over 6 years. From my observations, I can say that institutionalism is a spirit. I believe all forms of difficulties such as incarceration, homelessness, perversion and substance abuse, etc. have a spirit attached to them. If the curse is not broken, more than likely we will see repeated cases and these spirits would be passed on to the next generation. I challenge every inmate to overcome the **spirit of institutionalism.**

I also realize that many of the repeat offenders, although guilty of their crimes, are victims of circumstances. Oftentimes, there are hidden matters of the heart that are never dealt with. Your future may be going through the system of the courts, but God is watching over you. You can have freedom in your heart no matter how your case turns out.

This book was not written, by any means, to attack the inmate. It was written to open your eyes because you are valuable to God. I challenge you to go all the way with the Lord. Don't follow Him at a distance because the devil only needs a small space to destroy you. Get close to God and watch Satan flee.

The average inmate gets out of jail and goes directly to a family member who, in turn, supports them. The excitement of a loved one being released can quickly become stressful because it requires hard work to help this individual fit back into society and the experience, if not properly handled, can turn into a nightmare. Some families struggle with the transition because they lack the knowledge and skills to get to the root of the problem.

Do you have a loved one in jail? If so, do yourself a favor and read this book. It will serve as a resource in helping you to develop a life net between you and the inmate. If you are that loved one behind bars, I wrote this book specifically with you in mind. You will be challenged to pray, get involved, work together, find solutions to unanswered questions, address the issues and stop sweeping your problems under the rug.

Hopefully, this information will persuade you to allow God's unconditional love to touch your heart and change your life. God is a God of second chances. If you feel as if you have failed yourself, your family and your God, I want to inform you that you can get up again. **I command you in the name of Jesus to get up and get back in the race!** Deal with your mistakes and defeat your shame! If you don't deal with them *now*, they will mock you for the rest of your life.

CHAPTER ONE

Know This

Most inmates get out of jail without a real plan. They have an idea about what they want to pursue, but not a legitimate plan. In my dealing with inmates, I frequently come across those who are basically tired of being in jail. They have been in and out of jail all of their lives. I hear them say, "I can't do this anymore; this time has really taken its toll on me. I have a family." I hear the sincerity of their hearts but they are weak. I believe they really mean it, but they don't know what to do.

Their plan is unstructured and unfocused. They may say, "I'm going to get my life together and get a job," but once released, the first thing they do is take a vacation and go visit old friends. One inmate who had no plan at all ended right back in jail. When he was released from prison, there was no one to pick him up so he decided to *"borrow"* a nearby car to drive to the bus station. It was day one of his parole and already he was faced with auto theft charges.

A real plan starts with putting God first. This means becoming totally surrendered to God, growing in Him daily and trusting Him to direct your life. My first recommendation to any inmate is that they start attending a Christian fellowship in the jail so they can learn how to become totally surrendered to God. This will assist them in developing a relationship with God and build their faith. The next thing they must do is to accept Jesus Christ as their Lord and Savior. The following scriptures provide the basic steps to salvation for anyone.

> *"That if thou shalt confess with thy mouth the Lord Jesus, and shalt believe in thine heart that God hath raised him from the dead, thou shalt be saved." (Romans 10:10)*

"If we confess our sins, he is faithful and just to forgive us our sins, and to cleanse us from all unrighteousness."
(1 John 1:9)

To invite the Lord into your heart today, pray this simple prayer:

Lord, I acknowledge that I have done wrong and I ask you to forgive me for my sins. Lord, I believe that you died so I can be saved. I ask you to come into my heart and live there. Thank you for saving me today. Amen.

Now, thank God for your new life and begin living for him.

When a person says that they have accepted the Lord into their heart, they should expect some changes to occur. Let me point out three very important areas for change: integrity, conviction and repentance.

Integrity – is when a person becomes conscious of God to the point that they don't want to disappoint him, therefore, they strive to become trustworthy. It is similar to the integrity in a marriage. You cannot have a good marriage without trust nor can you have a good relationship with God without Him being able to trust you.

Conviction – is when a person has a fear and reverence for God. Every time they do something wrong or if think they have displeased or offended God, their conscience alerts them that it is not right and they proceed to get it right with God.

Repentance – becomes a way of life when a person is sorry for the wrong committed and they are compelled to seek forgiveness. Therefore a Christian is always examining their heart and confessing their sins before God when they feel guilty. Repentance is not seeking to see how much we can get away with and still go to heaven. On the contrary it is being quick to say, "I am sorry God for the things I have said or done."

It's okay for a person to accept the Lord when their back is against the wall. One's heart must be examined for sincerity so that growth can start immediately. Some will accept the Lord because they are scared and traumatized due to what has happened to them. Again, this is acceptable, however, they must be sure of their motive. God knows when someone is pretending to become religious in hopes that He will get them out of the mess they have gotten themselves into. True repentance consists of being genuine from the inside out. This is done in conjunction with developing a *relationship* with the Lord. If a person knows that something is wrong and he or she is struggling with guilt, I highly recommend that they seek the counsel of a mature Christian. Sometimes, even as a pastor, I find it necessary to clear my conscience by talking to someone.

Now, let's get on with the rest of the plan. Those who plan to succeed must become healed spiritually and emotionally. A major part of this healing process consists of communicating and exchanging information with a caseworker or counselor on a regular basis. It's also helpful to start a journal where you can write down your goals and ideas.

Your plan should also include becoming health conscious by eating right and exercising. This will relieve the stress and strengthen the physical mind. Attending self-help programs at the facility is another option. One cannot say that they trust God for direction in their life and do nothing about it. Remember, a person who does not plan will more than likely fail again. The devil's pitfall of failure can be avoided by **doing** what we say we are going to do.

One other aspect of the plan that is often overlooked is identifying a good church home outside of jail. Many inmates live a better Christian life while incarcerated than their family does on the outside.

I come in contact with inmates that attend at least two forms of worship per week while they are incarcerated. When they go home, most of their family members don't attend church that often or not at all. For that reason they cannot depend upon others for their spiritual direction. Initially they have to depend on others for money, food, shelter and transportation until they can get on their feet. Unfortunately, if this dependency is prolonged, it creates a temptation to fall back into sin. Some inmates will go back to ungodly sexual relationships that immediately stain their walk with God. So it is imperative for the newly released inmate to guard their heart. If your loved one returns home excited about God and wants to go to church frequently, don't call them a fanatic. Maybe God is trying to tell you something.

On the other hand, there are families that do attend church but their church may not offer what the inmate needs. When that is the case, the family should be open-minded and give their loved one space to choose a church where they will be better served. It is better for them to go to a fiery church and be nurtured than to be with the family and gradually lose interest because the church is not as lively as what they were introduced to in jail. I grant you, many churches are equipped to help you and your loved ones who are being released but you cannot approach this restoration period with a lackadaisical attitude.

As a family member, you should contact programs, churches, and any institution that will help. This should be done while they are incarcerated. If you don't know where to start, I recommend that you contact churches that have a prison ministry because those churches have knowledge of programs and job information to help men and women get back on their feet.

In interviewing inmates, I come across some that are better off going to a shelter or a halfway house for a while because the environment they are about to enter poses a problem. Take for example an inmate in one of my classes who was about to be released. He asked the judge to allow him to go to the Salvation Army, which has a six-week program to help people who are substance abusers. When he was told there would not be a vacancy for two weeks, he asked the judge if he could stay in jail until a vacancy became available. He was determined to enter the program because he knew he was not prepared to go back home. The judge commended him and granted him his request. Despite his fellow inmates who thought he was crazy for staying in jail, this inmate had a legitimate plan to get back on his feet. He saw the need to temporarily cut off family and friends until he got himself together. He told me that he could not celebrate his freedom until he was freed from those things that got him in trouble in the first place.

Recovery

Inmates should learn to fast and pray while incarcerated so that when they are released they will be trained to use self-control. They need to get accustomed to practicing this form of discipline because it will strengthen them to make wise decisions when it's time for them to enter back into society.

Inmates must be aware of the possibility of unfair treatments upon their release because society will not treat them with compassion and easily give them a chance. They must watch their reaction if people don't want to be bothered with them or if an employer turns them down when seeking employment. They must stay in tune with God because there will be times when much prayer will be needed to get through whatever obstacle the day brings. God is a God of second chances and they must seek him for direction because through prayer, doors will open.

In order for the family and the inmate to recover, everyone will need to walk in forgiveness. When this is done all inner hurts will be healed. Don't worry about fixing everything that is beyond human ability to correct. What you can't fix, **leave alone!**

Disillusion

I teach a bible class in maximum security, therefore most of the students that I deal with are in jail for a serious crime. I am constantly reminding them that just because they come to bible class and have given their life to God, they are not "out of the woods." Many of them go on trial and receive a sentence of 50 years or more. There are times when some of them become angry with God. They don't always understand that becoming a Christian while incarcerated means deliverance from the bondage of sin. It does not mean that they will automatically get out of jail. It is good that they have turned to the Lord but they must come to terms with the fact that they cannot bargain with God. I keep drilling and drilling in their minds that having God in their life is worth more than anything their future could possibly hold.

Praying For Your Loved Ones

One last major element of the plan that should be shared by both the inmate and the family is prayer.

I'm often asked by families to pray for their loved ones to be released from jail. This is not necessarily the most appropriate prayer, especially when the inmate is 100 percent guilty of the crime. If an inmate is out right guilty, you should pray for God's mercy in the situation. Pray that the ordeal will get their attention and that they will totally surrender to God. You should also pray that God's will be done over all court proceedings. This is the point where many inmates are at a crossroad and is the best time for God to get their attention. They may not get released physically but they can become released from the bondage of sin.

You may say that you don't know how to pray or what to pray. Just talk to God. Make it plain:

> "Heavenly Father I come to you in the name of Jesus on behalf of (name). I pray that you will have mercy on him. Although he has committed a crime don't let the courts treat him unfairly. Regardless of the outcome, I will give you the praise. Father, I also pray that you will get (name's) attention through this ordeal. I trust your faithfulness because you are a just God. Amen."

Prayer changes things. What the inmate will notice once they have established a consistent habit of prayer is that it will bring peace in their life.

Know this, you can have HIS PEACE through

prayer. This chapter has discussed the importance of an inmate having a plan to help them focus on how to live within the system and prepare for life on the outside. To recap, we could say that having a plan creates peace.

> **P**utting God first
> **E**xpecting a change of heart
> **A**llowing time for spiritual and emotional healing
> **C**onnecting with mentors and counselors
> **E**xercising and eating right

We also learned that having a plan requires surrendering our ways to His.

> **H**aving realistic expectations
> **I**dentifying a church home outside of jail
> **S**elf-control

It takes time to build a solid relationship with God. Get started on your plan today. Be determined to not settle for anything less than being completely delivered from the powers of Satan.

I am not saying give up on the person. You

should support your loved one as much as possible. It will also be wise to get a lawyer so that you will have someone to assist you with legal matters. A lawyer may be able to work out an alternative for those young and naive individuals. Some families struggle with whether to let them stay in jail and learn a lesson or pay the bond and get them out of the situation. I would advise any parent if it's a minor charge and its the first offense it would probably be better to get them out because a night or two is enough lesson for them. Some jails are so corrupted that it is not worth your child's future to let them stay and learn a lesson because they may come home and never be the same.

A WORD TO THE WISE

"If any of you lacks wisdom, he should ask God, who gives generously to all without finding fault, and it will be given to him." (James 1:5 NIV)

If this is new experience for you as a family I have provided the above verse. If you find yourself facing a loved one going to jail for the first time it no time to cast the blame or worry about what everybody is going to say when they find out what

Do You Have A Loved One In Jail?

has happened. There is a generous measure of wisdom that God has reserved for those that seek him in the time of trouble. It is a good time to take inventory of your life and come together as a family and ask God for directions. He will grant you wisdom in everything you are facing. Trouble has a way of strengthen families and bringing them closer to God. May that happen for you and your family is my prayer

CHAPTER TWO

Victims of Circumstance

According to Bureau of Justice statistics, at year-end 2002, 2,033,331 prisoners were held in Federal or State prisons and jails making the United States the world's top jailer. Of those two million inmates, nearly 900,000 of them were black men. Statistics show that there were 3,437 sentenced black male prisoners per 100,000 black males in the United States, compared to 1,176 sentenced Hispanic male inmates per 100,000 Hispanic males and 450 white male inmates per 100,000 white males. This book has not been written to black families only but you can clearly see that there are more black families impacted by this ordeal than others. At a time when there are five times as many black men in jail than there are enrolled in college we've got to take a closer look at the root cause. I repeat again, being locked-up is not solving the problems that our men and women are facing.

In surveying, I have found that most men who are in jail did not have a father that played an active role in their upbringing. When asked about their relationship with their father, I received one or more of the following responses:

1. My father is in jail.
2. My father is dead.
3. I don't know my father.
4. My father deserted me.
5. My mother and father are divorced.
6. My grandmother raised me.
7. My father has his own problems.

The above list provides the root cause of the problem. I have also concluded that most of them got into trouble because they were seeking for approval and acceptance that they did not get from their dads. When an inmate reconnects with his father and receives proper counseling; he has a very good chance of getting his life together.

As boys and girls grow up they need to be molded and shaped into adulthood by their parents. When that is missing they usually find false answers and hope in all the wrong places. Many of them will fall through the cracks.

The fallen victims:

- Many innocent individuals end up in jail because they were in the wrong place at the wrong time.
- Many young men and women tried the church before they got into trouble, but the church failed them for one reason or another.
- Many individuals get arrested without understanding their rights and often indite themselves because of ignorance.
- Many of them start taking drugs for depression, which may cause side affects, and often open doors for other problems that they will face while in jail and when they are eventually released.
- Many families can't pay the bond for those

who are eligible for it. Because most court cases are running behind schedule, a victim may stay in jail several months until their case is heard. It is possible for an inmate to be in jail close to a year before they go to trial. By the time justice is served they have suffered many forms of abuse from fellow inmates and/or the system. This ordeal may leave them traumatized and institutionalized.

Some get a bum-deal because many individuals who have already gone through the system have made it bad for the next person to be processed through the system.

- Many of them can't afford a good lawyer. Others wait too late to secure a court appointed lawyer and are left represented by someone who may not be best experienced for the job, therefore the inmate is penalized. If the lawyer is burnt out from a heavy workload the inmate may not get the attention they need in order for justice to be served.
- Many young men and women are victims of abuse because they have a history of poverty

and /or abandonment; therefore, they grow up resenting authority.

In some cases the inmate is guilty of the crime committed, however the circumstances centered on the crime are never brought to the light. Some lawyers are not as thorough as they should be by bringing forth the necessary witnesses or providing the all circumstances. This is known as lack of circumstantial evidence and is the contributing factor to why many victims get long-term sentences.

CHAPTER THREE

Forgiveness

*"If we confess our sins, he is faithful and just to **forgive** us our sins, and to cleanse us from all unrighteousness."*
(1 John 1:9)

It is very important for you as an individual to understand the power of forgiveness.

Forgiveness is God's way of showing us that He is merciful and that He loves us un-conditionally. As human beings we often love others based upon conditions such as loving those who love us and doing a favor for those who will return one. We have concluded that God operates in the same manner. Satan is responsible for this confusion. He is your enemy and he doesn't want you to receive God's forgiveness. If you lack understanding in this area, the devil will keep you in bondage by making you think that God will never forgive you. Confusion is a major reason why millions of people do not embrace salvation or enjoy the freedom of forgiveness that Jesus purchased for us on the cross. As you seek forgiveness for your sins, it is necessary to forgive others. I have the privilege, as a prison minister, to counsel hundreds of inmates and help them obtain forgiveness. It brings me joy to watch Satan's power be broken off their lives. I want to share four actual cases that I have personally dealt with where each individual was set free from unforgiveness. The names have been changed to ensure privacy.

Case 1:

Robert was a young man who had strayed away from church and his life took a downward turn. He was in and out of jail and eventually got into serious trouble. The prison chaplain assigned me to minister at maximum security and the first person on my list was Robert.

Robert had just rededicated his life to God and signed up for a mentor. He had been in jail about a year before we met. He was charged with murder but he insisted that he only killed a man to protect his life. Robert's claim of self-defense did not convince the prosecuting attorney who was working hard to convict him of murder. The devil had already done a job on Robert's mind; therefore, he was a challenge for me. He was worried about whether he could be completely forgiven because he had taken someone's life. He was traumatized with what had happened and had become very restless. The only comfort that helped ease his mind was that the mother of the deceased man was a Christian and she was very forgiving during the ordeal.

It took several visits for me to get him to a place where I could minister to him. Eventually, I won his trust and he was ready to receive what I had to say. I made him aware that I was not there as a lawyer or a judge but as a minister of the gospel. I shared with him about God's unconditional love. I made him aware of the fact that even if he had killed a man out of pure hatred and not self-defense there was still room for him to receive forgiveness from the Almighty God. Once I closed the door of guilt I was able to help him experience the freedom that he was seeking by leading him into a prayer of forgiveness. I proceeded to make him understand that God's love is based upon His grace and mercy and not upon our self-righteousness. We cannot become righteous enough to earn God's grace. It is a gift. It is not that we are worthy of it; it is all because God is merciful.

Robert had been to his preliminary hearing but his trial had not yet taken place. Over the months we had many visits and prayers together. There were times when he had a relapse and I had to repeat some of the things I had told him earlier. As time went on, I could see that God was doing a work in him. As he continued to walk with God his stress level began to drop and we had more time to talk about the Bible rather than about his problems.

Finally, Robert went to court and was sentenced to 10 years in prison, with four years suspended. We have stayed in touch and are pen pals. Although he is in prison, Robert is still growing as a Christian and he realizes that it's his relationship with God that has set him free. Robert now has less that a year left. He took up a trade to make himself marketable upon his release from prison. I am very proud of Robert. He also feels that God has a calling on his life for the ministry.

If you feel as if you have done too much evil for God to forgive you, pray this prayer:

> Father, I thank you because you are a God that loves everybody. I understand that you don't like everything we do as a person but you love us as your creation. I thank you that you created me for your purpose and love me in spite of what I have done. Father I pray that you will forgive me and cleanse me from all the wrong in my life. I forgive others and myself. Thank you for loving me enough to let me pray this prayer and let me know that I have not done too much evil for you to forgive me. This I ask in Jesus' name. Amen!

Case 2:

Randy was enjoying a quiet night a home and had no interest in going out. His best friend, Bruce, dropped by and persuaded him to go joyriding. The night led to mischief and the two got into a fight. Randy was killed. Bruce was burdened with guilt because he blamed himself for Randy's death. His shame was intensified when he had to face Randy's mom and tell her what happened.

With the help of the Holy Spirit, I led Bruce into a prayer that released him from the tragic incident that occurred on the night of his friend's death. I explained to Bruce that he had to forgive himself before he could receive God's forgiveness. The minute Bruce repeated the prayer he said it felt like a ton of bricks lifted off his chest. God took his sins and threw them into the sea never to be remembered. I instructed him to not allow the devil to make him feel guilty and take that burden up again. I shared the following scriptures with him.

"He will turn again, he will have compassion upon us; he will subdue our iniquities; and thou wilt cast all

their sins into the depths of the sea." (Micah 7:19)

"I, even I, am he that blotteth out thy transgressions for my own sake, and will not remember thy sins." (Isaiah 43:25)

Bruce continued counseling with me until he was sentenced to prison. God prepared him for what was ahead and he left encouraged to walk with God.

If you are having a hard time forgiving yourself, pray this prayer:

> Father, I thank you that you have delivered Bruce and I thank you because you will do the same for me. I release my fears and hurts to you. I forgive myself for the wrong that I have held deep in my heart. I cast it off in Jesus name. Father I ask you to forgive me for the pain that I have caused others. Thank you that all my sins are cast into the depths of the sea

forever in Jesus' name. Amen.

Case 3:

Michael and James were the best of friends. They grew up together and always shared everything. If one had, that meant they both had. Michael, for some reason always seemed to have more money to spend. What James didn't know was that Michael sold drugs to earn his extra cash.

One evening while they were riding in James's car, the cops pulled them over for a traffic violation and decided to conduct a search. Before Michael got out of the car he managed to slip some drugs under the seat in James's car. The drugs were found and James, being the owner of the vehicle, was blamed. James was not only faced with a traffic violation, but with possession of drugs. Michael had a previous police record, which James was aware of, but not knowing the full extent of it. Michael was guilty of possession and hiding the drugs in his buddy's automobile but would not admit it.

The two were placed in jail; they were separated and unable to communicate during the entire process while they awaited the outcome of the case.

Eventually they were face to face in court. Michael's family secured a good lawyer on his behalf, who put together a good defense for him. James's family was disappointed in him for choosing to continue to hang with Michael after their many warnings. Therefore they did not help him obtain a lawyer. James settled for a court-appointed lawyer. In the courtroom, Michael betrayed his buddy and would not confess to hiding the drugs. He lied on James to save himself. With the help of his lawyer he received no jail time, only probation. James was sentenced to six years with the judge suspending four years. As James listened to everything in disbelief, he could not believe Michael would not stand up for him. As James was led away, Michael only stared at the floor.

After being in jail for a while, James became very bitter. He had difficulty accepting what his buddy did to him and he was also hurt that his family did not support him like Michael's family did. His stress and agony caused him to turn to God. For some, going to jail has its benefits: it is a good opportunity for a person to meet God, get their GED, learn a trade or earn college credits. God has also raised many chaplains and dedicated volunteers from jail.

It was not by accident that James stumbled into my Bible class when I was teaching on forgiveness. It was by divine intervention (the will of God). That's why it is good to pray for your loved ones in jail and pray for those who are on the front line ministering to them. I did not know anything about James or his problem, but God did. I am only God's mouthpiece in the jail. As I taught, God began to deal with James. He was amazed that God was speaking to him through me. He became broken. He opened up and began to discuss what was bothering him for many months. In my experience, the minute a person opens up, God gives me what to say to them so that they can be delivered. God's grace and mercy is very powerful. As James talked I noticed the bitterness on the inside of him. I immediately prayed with him to be released from it. I read the following scripture to him.

> *"Let all bitterness, and wrath, and anger, and clamour, and evil speaking, be put away from you, with all malice." (Ephesians 4:31)*

The next thing we dealt with was forgiveness. In order for James to be healed from his wounds he needed to forgive those whom he felt had deserted and betrayed him. We read the following:

> *"And when ye stand praying, forgive, if ye have aught against any: that your Father also which is in heaven may forgive you your trespasses. But if ye do not forgive, neither will your Father which is in heaven forgive you your trespasses." (Mark 11:25-26)*

I led James into a prayer of forgiveness, making sure that he had not only forgiven all those individuals but that he had forgiven himself.

We also prayed a prayer of thanksgiving for God's grace using this scripture:

> *"But he giveth more grace. Wherefore he saith, God resisteth the proud, but giveth grace unto the humble. Submit yourselves therefore to God. Resist the devil, and he will flee from you." (James 4:6-7)*

Because I knew that the devil was going to test James about his deliverance. I taught him how to resist the devil. I also wanted him to know that God was there to continue to give him grace so he could go on with his life.

If you are dealing with bitterness, pray this prayer:

> Father, I thank you that I don't have to live another day with bitterness. I release all bitterness, anger and grudges that I hold against those that have hurt me. I put it away from me in the name of Jesus. Amen

Case 4:

Peter was a professional drug dealer; having sold drugs most of his life. One day he received a tip that one of his opponents was going to be killed. Because he hated the person and recognized that it would mean less competition for him with the person dead, he did not warn him. Ultimately, Peter was arrested for drug charges and while in jail, he gave his life to the Lord.

As time went on I met Peter. He was a faithful student in my Bible class. I eventually got around to teaching on forgiveness as I normally do and Peter, with his renewed heart, was struggling with guilt. He knew that a person was about to be killed and because of his own selfishness, he did not help the person. He was wondering if he could be completely forgiven since he could not bring the person back to life to apologize for being so ruthless. I instructed him to forgive himself and ask God to forgive him. I also made him aware that although God could not undo his mistake, he could be released from bondage because Christ died for all of our sins. I made sure he understood that when we can't fix something that means God wants us to leave it alone. Peter was delivered that night and left my class with tears of joy knowing that he didn't have to live under that burden any longer.

If you have killed someone or have any type of involvement in someone's death, pray this prayer.

> Father, I thank you for giving me a second chance. Please forgive me for harming your creation. You are the giver of life. I am truly sorry for my

actions. I forgive myself so that I can receive your forgiveness. Please take away the guilt and shame that I feel for the death of (victim) in the name of Jesus. I thank you for setting me free today; this is my prayer in Jesus' name. Amen!

Blasphemy

Perhaps you can identify with one of the individuals in the cases you just read and want to experience God's forgiveness in your life. Maybe you're thinking, "but what about me? I'm a serial killer. I raped several women. Is there hope for me?" The answer is still YES. As long as a person repents and turns from their wicked ways, they will receive forgiveness. Even if a person blasphemes God, He allows forgiveness for them as well.

Blasphemy is any act that insults, shows contempt or lack of reverence for God. Here is a sampling of blaspheming activities:

1. Satanic worship
2. Occultism

3. Abortion
4. Homosexuality
5. Trans-sexual operation
6. Suicide bombers
7. Assisting someone to commit suicide because they are terminally ill
8. Same-sex marriages
9. The ordination of gay men and women as ministers of the gospel
10. Vandalizing and robbing God's church

There are many more blaspheming activities other than those listed above. No matter how evil they may be, they can be corrected with proper counsel and acceptance of salvation. Although some involvement with sin may scar a person worse than others, there is always an opportunity for deliverance.

I close this chapter with my favorite example of God's forgiveness. It's a story of a man called Saul of Tarsus in the New Testament of our Bible. Saul was an unbeliever. He hated Christians and because he lacked the truth about Jesus Christ and the gospel, he fought against the church of God. He used his energy to interfere with God's people, going out of his way to have them jailed or stoned to death. He operated very boldly against the Holy Ghost until he had an encounter with Jesus. Stricken by blindness, he desperately followed Jesus' instructions to receive forgiveness and was delivered from his sins. After his conversion, Saul changed his name to Paul and committed the rest of his life to teaching the gospel. You can find the account on Saul in the following verses in the bible:

> *"And Saul, yet breathing out threatenings and slaughter against the disciples of the Lord, went unto the high priest, And desired of him letters to Damascus to the synagogues, that if he found any of this way, whether they were men or women, he might bring them bound unto Jerusalem. And as he journeyed, he came near Damascus: and suddenly there shined round about him a light from heaven: And he fell to the earth, and heard a voice saying unto him, Saul, Saul, why persecutest thou me? And he said, Who art thou, Lord? And the Lord*

said, I am Jesus whom thou persecutest: it is hard for thee to kick against the pricks. And he trembling and astonished said, Lord, what wilt thou have me to do? And the Lord said unto him, Arise, and go into the city, and it shall be told thee what thou must do." (Acts 9:1-6)

"Then Ananias answered, Lord, I have heard by many of this man, how much evil he hath done to thy saints at Jerusalem: And here he hath authority from the chief priests to bind all that call on thy name. But the Lord said unto him, Go thy way: for he is a chosen vessel unto me, to bear my name before the Gentiles, and kings, and the children of Israel: For I will shew him how great things he must suffer for my name's sake." (Acts 9:13-16)

Saul had actually blasphemed God by persecuting Christians. If God forgave Saul and placed him on the right road, he will do the same for you and anyone that calls upon his name.

CHAPTER FOUR

Sick and Tired of Being Sick and Tired

No one is going to do for you what you need to do for yourself. If you find yourself on a merry-go-round, in and out of jail, you need to wake-up and come to the realization that only God will give you the grace to do what you think you cannot do. That is why the scripture says. *"I can do all things through Christ, which strengtheneth me." (Philippians 4:13)*

Do You Have A Loved One In Jail?

Certainly you are tired and exhausted. You were probably suffering from burnout before you got arrested. Haven't you given too much of your time to the jail system? Can you afford to give away anymore valuable time?

Why Sit Here Until We Die?

Some people find themselves in the midst of hard times and it seems like there is no light at the end of the tunnel. Years have passed by and you have nothing to show for them. You may be in jail holding a pity party wondering if there is any hope for a person such as yourself? You may have also said, "What's the use?" But at the same time you are sick and tired of your situation. Before you can get out of what you are in, you need to ask yourself this most important question – Why sit here and die? Dying is not the answer for you. Dying to some is only a form of giving up. I challenge you to change your thinking. You may not be able to change your circumstances but you can change your mind. This can be done through the process of elimination. Eliminate every negative thought you have been holding onto. Move closer to God and let him work for you because answers are locked up on the inside of you.

Here's a story from the Old Testament that helps illustrate this principle.

Four men found themselves in a dilemma; no one could help them because everyone was impacted by a famine in the land. The men made up their minds that before dying of starvation they would at least try to seek the help of others. Their determination turned into a miracle.

> *"And there were four leprous men at the entering in of the gate: and they said one to another, Why sit we here until we die? If we say, we will enter into the city, then the famine is in the city, and we shall die there: and if we sit still here, we die also. Now therefore come, and let us fall unto the host of the Syrians: if they save us alive, we shall live; and if they kill us, we shall but die. And they rose up in the twilight, to go unto the camp of the Syrians: and when they were come to*

the uttermost part of the camp of Syria, behold, there was no man there. For the Lord had made the host of the Syrians to hear a noise of chariots, and a noise of horses, even the noise of a great host: and they said one to another, Lo, the king of Israel hath hired against us the kings of the Hittites, and the kings of the Egyptians, to come upon us. Wherefore they arose and fled in the twilight, and left their tents, and their horses, and their asses, even the camp as it was, and fled for their life." (2Kings 7:3-7)

Notice that the leprous men went through a process of elimination. They eliminated the places that would have brought absolute destruction to them first. Then they considered what they had left. The only sign of hope carried a risk but they agreed that it was their only chance of survival.

Once God saw that their hearts were innocent and that they were seeking a better life for themselves, He had mercy on them. God used leprous men that people had written off as "nobody" to bring deliverance to Israel.

Let's take a closer look at the wording in fourth verse of this scripture:

> "...*if they save us alive, we shall live; and if they **kill** us, we shall but die.*"

The word "kill" is used because there is a difference between getting killed and dying. To die meant that they would do nothing but just sit around in their comfort zone or return to the city and wait for the worst. To get killed meant that they would only die after they had exhausted all possibilities. Since death was sure to come they decided to experiment with possibility. The wonderful thing about possibility is chance. Chance meant that they had a 50-50 percent chance of dying or living. In their case, it brought them life. In less than 24 hours they were filled and had enough food to save the city.

God is watching you. He is measuring your level of determination and your ability to dream. Keep dreaming because when God opens the door you will need to put some action behind your dreams and God will bless it. Psalms 1:3; states, "whatsoever he doeth shall prosper." Dreaming is only a motivator, but **doing** is what causes miracles to happen.

There's an old expression that says, "If you want to get what you've never had, you'll have to do what you've never done." Don't sit and rot behind a prison wall with your future locked up on the inside of you. This is not the end of you. You are only clay in the Master's hand. Ask Him to mold and make you over again. The initial process is going to be painful, but you need to pressure yourself into doing what you don't feel like doing until you break through the barrier.

If you are sick and tired and know that you are at the end of your road, pray this prayer:

> Father, I am tired of trying to make it without you. I cannot make it on my own. Forgive me for being stubborn. I submit myself to your will. I give myself to you to be molded and made into the person you want me to be. I am sick and tired of my ways. Please help me today. Send someone that I can talk to who will help me move beyond where I am. Soften my heart to

hear you. Whichever way you chose to speak to me, have your way Lord. I thank you for loving me and I am confident that you have done what I have asked you to do in Jesus name. Amen!

CHAPTER FIVE

Are You Under A Load?

Hopefully you just prayed the prayer from the previous chapter because you are sick and tired of being sick and tired and want a change in your life. If you are like most inmates I come across, you're probably under a load because you think you are the only one who is experiencing trouble. Trouble knows no name or address. A negative reaction to trouble will wear anyone down and take a toll on an individual mentally and physically.

> *"We are troubled on every side, yet not distressed; we are perplexed, but not in despair; Persecuted, but not*

forsaken; cast down, but not destroyed." (2 Corinthians 4:8-9)

In order to get from under a load and free yourself from excess baggage you must be willing to go through a process. I'm going to use another story from the Old Testament to help develop this thought.

"So they two went until they came to Bethlehem. And it came to pass, when they were come to Bethlehem, that all the city was moved about them, and they said, Is this Naomi? And she said unto them, Call me not Naomi, call me Mara: for the Almighty hath dealt very bitterly with me. I went out full, and the Lord hath brought me home again empty: why then call ye me Naomi, seeing the Lord hath testified against me, and the Almighty hath afflicted me?" (Ruth 1:19-21)

In the book of Ruth, Elimelech along with his wife, Naomi moved their family from Bethlehem to

Moab to make a better living. As the years went on Elimelech died leaving his wife and two sons to survive in the midst of hard times. The boys got married and shortly afterward they died too. Now this leaves Naomi and her two daughters-in-law to provide for themselves. After assessing her losses and realizing that she was not getting any younger, Naomi decided to return home to Bethlehem. Knowing that it would not be an easy journey she encouraged her daughters-in-law to return to their own people and she would travel by herself. Ruth refused to leave her mother-in-law while Orpah decided to take her mother-in-law's advice and went back home.

Naomi was worn and under a load. Upon her arrival back to her country she instructed the people to call her "Mara" because she felt like everything was against her. You cannot base everything on how you feel. Satan, if allowed, has a way of getting the best of us through our thinking. If you think wrong you are also going to believe wrong. What Naomi was thinking was not what God was thinking. When you are under a load you have a tendency to think the worse because your ways are not like His ways. Neither are your thoughts like his. (Isaiah 55:8-9)

I believe if Ruth had not accompanied Naomi, the load of her frustrations and disappointments would have caused her to sink into a deep depression. Ruth gave Naomi something to live for.

God knows exactly what you are going through and He has already revealed it to someone else. God is so gracious. When He is determined to bless you, He will place someone in your life that will help bring out the best in you.

Many inmates are single, all alone with no family, friends or loved ones. It seems that all they had to live for is gone. Many have actually stopped living, but merely exist from day to day. Mentally they have given up on life. You cannot allow how you feel to determine your future. Before it's too late, take the necessary steps to get from under your load.

Five Steps To Get From Under A Load

1. Bury The Past

You must rise up over the things of your past such as struggles, tragedies and defeated thinking.

Your future is waiting for you. Stop trying to take the old into the new. *"Neither do men put new wine into old bottles: else the bottles break, and the wine runneth out, and the bottles perish, but they put new wine into new bottles, and both are preserved." (Matthew 9:17)*

Actions put life into what we say. We must not only speak it, we must become doers of the word of God. Paul in his writings said, *"I think myself happy." (Acts 26:2)*

2. Break The Ties

Ties are hindrances that you need to turn loose in order to grow so that God can bless you. You may be asking God to forgive you but unwilling to forgive someone else. That is a tie that needs to be broken because as long as you are unwilling to forgive a person you are tied to them. Another tie that could bind you is the misconception in your mind. Sometimes we have to change our thinking before we can receive what God has for us.

Naomi and Elimelech lived during the period of the judges and because there was no prophet or king everyone did what was right in their own eyes.

To move from Bethlehem seemed like it was the right thing to do but it was not God's will. While Bethlehem represented the house of bread or the "will of God," Moab represented the complete opposite. Therefore Naomi needed to break the tie if she wanted to be blessed. As long as she remained in Moab she was going to stay in bondage. She rose up and got out of Moab and went back home.

You may be locked in but you are not locked out from the presence of God. The bars that you are behind symbolize a tangible bondage but that does not control your mental and spiritual freedom. Rise up in your mind and break the ties to whatever is holding you back. You have to be challenged to be strong. The initial process may seem hard or worthless but it is necessary for your growth. I am challenging you to get up and take action in your mind.

3. Face Reality

Naomi had dreamed of going back to her people and regaining her property. When she heard how the Lord had blessed her country by sending it the much needed rain and how their wheat and barley crops were producing in abundance, she faced reality. She could no longer live in denial; she knew it was time for her to go back home. She did not allow her past to cheat her out of the good that was in store for her. Naomi understood she had a choice to make; she could either stay in Moab as a beggar or return to Bethlehem as a citizen. Either choice proved to be a test for her. However, going back to Bethlehem meant going back to her true place of worship. Hearing what God had done for her country made her sensitive to God's grace. Hearing stimulated her faith. *"So then faith cometh by hearing, and hearing by the word of God." (Romans 10:17)* Many inmates waste precious time watching television, playing cards or sleeping all day. Some pass up classes and other productive activities just to sit around and joke with their peers. There's nothing wrong with socializing but you should have limits. There are a number of things you can do to help yourself. Come up with a "things to do list" and take advantage of your day. Do some soul-searching and assess your skills. Establish some boundaries for yourself. Define who you are as a person. Determine what you want to do with your life. Keep some form of a journal in order to set up a schedule and set a deadline. Always question yourself by establishing why your happiness or peace is important to you. Coming to terms with yourself is how you face reality. Once you've made this assessment, you can recognize a good opportunity when it knocks at your door.

4. Test Those Who Say They Are With You

As discussed earlier, Naomi made her daughters-in-law aware of what they would face if they decided to journey back to Bethlehem with her. She was prepared to return home by herself if necessary.

Orpah was not willing to face all that was ahead of them and decided that it made sense to go back to her people. Ruth was a woman of faith. She placed Naomi's needs above her own. Although she realized that clinging to Naomi meant that she might never get married and have children, Ruth also wanted to maximize her life. When you go after the maximum you must separate yourself from those who settle for the minimum.

As an inmate you should constantly test your peers to determine if they are on the same level of thinking as you are. Some people will drain you out of every ounce of faith you can muster. Don't hang around people that don't have visions, goals or purpose. You cannot afford to allow people to discourage or keep you from reaching your full potential.

5. Persevere

> *"So they two <u>went until they came to Bethlehem.</u> And it came to pass, when they were come to Bethlehem, that all the city was moved about them, and they said, Is this Naomi?" (Ruth 1:19)*

It had to have been a demanding trip for Naomi and Ruth. The land of Moab is located to the southeast of Bethlehem across the Dead Sea. There were hills and mountains to climb. There may have been robbers and rapists along the way, not to mention the wild beasts and other unknown dangers. Naomi started out bitter but as she persevered her attitude about life began to change; she did not allow any obstacle to stand in her way. I'm sure the people stared at them as they entered the city. People have a way of making you feel awkward.

The pressure and stress that the two were under represent the oppositions you will face as you go through life. God is with you as you go through the fire. He promised that it would not burn you (Isaiah 43:2). Where did these women get the strength to do what they did? It was divine intervention that preserved them and helped them to make it home. When you say you are going to do something and you do it, it builds confidence in your heart so that the next time an obstacle shows up, you have the assurance to persevere right through to the finish.

CHAPTER SIX

Pressured To Perform

Many of you reading this book at one time had things going well, however, you are now experiencing difficulty. Maybe you are under a lot of pressure because what you are facing is more like a nightmare. You would not have imagined in a million years that you would be in your current situation. I pray that you will get a deeper hunger for God and rise to a more purposeful life and take back what the devil has stolen from you. You may think, "How can I rise to a purposeful life considering where I am?" You have to make the best of your circumstances because even in jail there are small opportunities that knock at your door from time to time. It may be a program you can attend or a job assignment in your block. My point is that you need to pay attention to the crack in the door. God has a way of causing small things to turn into something grand.

Let's go back to the book of Ruth and study the following scriptures:

> *"Turn again, my daughters, go your way; for I am too old to have an husband. If I should say, I have hope, if I should have an husband also tonight, and should also bear sons; Would ye tarry for them till they are grown? Would ye stay for them from having husbands? Nay, my daughters; for it grieveth me much for your sakes that the hand of the Lord is gone out against me. And they lifted up their voice, and wept again: and Orpah kissed her mother-in-law; but Ruth clave unto her." (Ruth 1:12-14)*

Naomi was facing immense pressure after the death of her husband and two sons. She told her two daughters-in-law that she was too old to remarry and have sons for them to wed according to their custom. If she had attempted to do that, she would have put her daughters-in-law and herself under extreme pressure. Instead she turned the matter over to God and released them from feeling obligated to stay with her. By releasing them, she gave God an opportunity to work a miracle on her behalf. When you have reached your limit, do like Naomi, take your hands out of it and let God have his way.

Ruth clung to Naomi because she saw that God was in the midst of her life. She also realized that her future was somehow connected to Naomi. The two women were instrumental in helping each other reach their destiny. Naomi taught Ruth how to worship and Ruth began to esteem the God of her country more than the doctrines of Moab. Ruth gave Naomi the moral support she needed that helped her overcome bitterness.

God recognized Ruth's loyalty to her mother-in-law, and as a result, He rewarded her with a husband and honored her with a son. Who would have thought that Ruth would marry a wealthy man, become the great-grand mother of the famous King David and the ancestress of Jesus Christ?

How To Handle Pressure

For the most part, the pressure you are feeling is a battle of the mind. This is a state of confusion and restlessness where a person does not know what to do or believe anymore. Mind battles often occur when you are unsure about personal things you struggle with and there is no one to talk to about it. It is in this vulnerable condition, that Satan will try to confuse your thinking towards God and life if you allow him. Without clarity, the devil will attack the mind with everything that is far from the truth. Please note that God is knocking at your heart. You must stand strong and draw closer to Him. *"Draw nigh to God, and he will draw nigh to you. Cleanse your hands, ye sinners; and purify your hearts, ye double minded." (James 4:8)* The closer you get to God, the easier you will find it to cleanse yourself from those things that have stained your conscience and disrupted your peace of mind.

Overcoming mental pressure is a daily battle, but if you make an effort to put God first, you will experience His peace and your life will begin to gradually fall back into place.

As you strive to get a grip on life you could find

yourself overwhelmed and pressured because of the environment you are in. Keep in mind that your future is at stake. Look out for yourself! Your peers may not sense the urgency that you are sensing to get your life together; therefore you must look to the source that is greater than your problem. That source is Jesus. Please meditate on the next scriptures and know that God will be with you like He was with these individuals:

> *"And the Lord said unto him, Surely I will be with thee, and thou shalt smite the Midianites as one man." (Judges 6:16)*

> *"And the Lord said unto Gideon, The people that are with thee are too many for me to give the Midianites into their hands, lest Israel vaunt themselves against me saying, Mine own hand hath saved me." (Judges 7:2)*

> *"And the Lord said unto Gideon, By the three hundred men that lapped will I save you, and deliver the Midianites*

into thine hand: and let all the other people go every man unto his place." (Judges 7:7)

"And all this assembly shall know that the Lord saveth not with sword and spear: for the battle is the Lord's, and he will give you into our hands." (1 Samuel 17:47)

"And he answered, Fear not: for they that be with us are more than they that be with them." (2 Kings 6:16)

"Ye shall not need to fight in this battle: set yourselves, stand ye still, and see the salvation of the Lord with you, O Judah and Jerusalem: fear not, nor be dismayed; tomorrow go out against them: for the Lord will be with you." (2 Chronicles 20:17)

If you are struggling with feelings of pressure, it might be because you are empty and void of God's word. I challenge you to set aside time each day to pray and read the Bible. You may not be able to comprehend everything you are reading, but get started. Eventually, you will develop a love for His word.

CHAPTER 7

The Silent Frustration of Masturbation

Over the last couple chapters we have talked a lot about the mind. You have been asked to change your mind and way of thinking – challenge your mind –renew your mind—overcome the battles of your mind. Everything about you is tied to the mind, including your spiritual freedom. Where you are spiritually or carnally will affect every aspect of your life. Most of all, it affects how you deal with human sexuality. The average person will never come forth and admit that they are struggling sexually. This silent frustration turns into guilt (Satan loves to attack the mind with guilt) and it keeps you from trying to build a solid relationship with God. However, God is omniscient. He is all knowing. That means that there is *nothing* about you, even what goes on in your so-called secret closet, that goes unnoticed by Him.

As a result of my many years of prison ministry and hundreds of consultations, I felt it was imperative to address an issue that is on the minds of many. The number one question that I am asked by Christian inmates is, "Is masturbation a sin?"

The Truth About Masturbation

Masturbation is an act or by-product of the carnal mind and since having a carnal mind is against the will of God, we can assume that masturbation *is* a sin and that it displeases God. The following scriptures support this argument:

> *"For they that are after the flesh do mind the things of the flesh; but they that are after the Spirit the things of the Spirit. For to be carnally minded is death; but to be spiritually minded is life and peace. Because the carnal*

> *mind is enmity against God: for it is not subject to the law of God neither, indeed, can be. So, then they that are in the flesh cannot please God. But ye are not in the flesh, but in the Spirit, if so be that the Spirit of God dwell in you. Now if any man have not the Spirit of Christ, he is none of his."* (Romans 8:5-9)

On the contrary, God does not want me to beat you over the head and sentence you to hell without ministering to you. An alarming number of people whether single, married, male, female, Christians, non-Christians, inmates or people in the general society practice masturbation often.

Masturbation is a personal issue; those who engage in it do it for different reasons and they view it differently. Getting free is going to take a process. If you don't get free immediately don't become discouraged. You may need to resolve other issues in your life before you can fully overcome masturbation. Let's take a look at a few possible motives for masturbation and then we'll discuss some solutions.

(Please note, because my prison ministry focuses on the male inmate, I have limited my discussion to men on this subject).

10 Reasons Why Men May Become Tempted To Masturbate

1. **Conversations:** Conversations often stimulate the mind to do things it hears. Men have a tendency to talk about sex when they are together. This can trigger masturbation to enter a person's life just based on what they have heard others say. You need to guard your ears from what you hear and watch what you allow to come out of your mouth. *"Unto the pure all things are pure: but unto them that are defiled and unbelieving is nothing pure; but even their mind and conscience is defiled." (Titus 1:15)*
2. **Pictures and Magazines:** Images that a person see will basically turn them on. We feed off of what we see. Adult magazines are popular in jail cells. If you look at pornographic pictures for long periods of time, sooner or later you will want to gratify your-

self by fantasizing that you are involved with the person on the pages. Certainly, it is not easy for an inmate to throw a magazine away. However, after reading this book I pray that you will eventually get there because that is what you're going to need to do in order to close the door.

3. **Wet dreams:** A dream is a product of our subconscious mind. We usually dream about things that are relative to us. Rarely do we dream about things that are unrelated to us. Even when we are experiencing a nightmare, it is generally linked to our personality, emotion, or past. A wet dream is something that every male experiences. Although it's a little messy, it's enjoyable. It is messy because we have little tolerance for semen once it leaves our body. We often wish the dreams were longer and more frequent. God has designed us with a sperm bank and when it is filled to its capacity, if we don't have an ejaculation, we will have a wet dream. This tempts some to take it further and masturbate once they wake up. Some might ask, "well if a wet dream is a

part of nature, what's wrong with masturbation?" You should take the blame if you were not guarding your spirit by watching X-rated movies or involved in some form of pornography before going to sleep. If that was the case, you need to repent for your actions. Your actions before you retire for the night can trigger a dream. If your heart condemns you, repent (1 John 3:20). Don't ever struggle with when to repent. Whenever you feel guilty about something, seek forgiveness. When you guard your spirit and set high standards you might wake up wet, but vaguely remember the dream. If you are married you will mostly dream about your spouse. This is not a set rule, but most likely. Many factors can make this very different for you. You must take into consideration your background and your level of maturity as a Christian.

4. **Prolonged Erections:** Men usually wake up to an erection in the morning before going to the bathroom. This continues until later in life. Older men experience fewer erections but do not lose their ability to

have an erection and especially to masturbate. Having an erection can become embarrassing to a man if someone notices it. It also can be an ego booster. This is the most tempting time for men to handle themselves. As an inmate it is best to keep your clothes on in your cell as much as possible and you may be less tempted to experiment with yourself.

5. **Childhood Habit:** Boys begin to notice changes in their bodies at different ages. They spend hours in the mirror watching and experimenting with their body and its function. Boys become curious about their ability to release semen. They are curious about the length of their penis and if it has grown lately. Every boy has probably pulled out a tape measure and measured his penis several times in life. This often leads to masturbation. Being curious about his first wet dream can also tempt a boy to start pulling on his penis. These passions make him want to keep doing it and then he finds himself locked into a long-term habit.

6. **Anger, Frustration and Resentment:**

Masturbation is a reaction of your emotions. As teenagers, boys find themselves learning to masturbate when they become angry or frustrated with their parents or peers. It is used as a way of protecting and rewarding ones self when feeling like no one cares or understands. This reaction can follow teens into their adult years and every time they get into a quarrel with their mate or an associate, they turn to them self for self-gratification. Once this act sets in, it is hard to stop. Most inmates deal with many forms of anger, frustration and resentment. These three emotions have opened the door wide for them to indulge in masturbation.

7. **Loneliness:** When it seems like there is no one in this world to trust, most inmates go into isolation. Isolation is when a person is in a vulnerable state and needs help, but too proud to admit it. Isolation is also a form of dissatisfaction that will cause a person to seek fulfillment in a way that is known as "solo-sex." Masturbation will slowly rob you of portions of intimacy that you should

experience as a Christian. Please continue to strive for purity because eventually you will learn more about your secret struggles and develop ways to defeat the devil. Some inmates are completely free from masturbation while others have a long way to go. No one needs to know where you are in this process. Keep it as your prayer request to God and keep going.

8. **Idle Time In Bed:** It is time to open your eyes and see the set-up. If you are in bed and experiencing an erection from something that you are getting gratification from; the constant rubbing or touching yourself will lead you down that familiar road. You need to get out of bed and get dressed; otherwise you are going to satisfy yourself. Pay attention to your routine. You may need to stay up later, go to bed on a lighter stomach, sing songs unto the Lord, or whisper prayers to Him to help occupy your mind.

9. **Lust:** Men in particular are very good at using their eyes to pick up on things that most females don't have a clue as to how fast we are. Because of our sex drive and

imagination, when a man sees a woman — in a flash— he has checked out her breasts, hips, thighs, and legs without her knowing about it. Lusting after women can link to fantasizing, which often tempts one to masturbate. *"For all that is in the world, the lust of the flesh, and the lust of the eyes, and the pride of life, is not of the Father, but is of the world." (I John 2:16)*

10. **Lingering Thoughts:** You can test your vulnerability by your thought pattern. If it is a passing thought you are not in a danger zone. If it is a lingering thought you **are** in a danger zone and about to fall into sin. Once the devil has sown a thought in your mind and you continually meditate on it, you will soon crave to feed your flesh. Usually, when a man is feeling lustful and determined to indulge in himself, he gets the Vaseline, lotion and a towel. At this point, it is too late, and the man will empty his sperm bank. Satan is very clever, so be careful of daydreaming and impure thoughts. *"Casting down imaginations, and every high thing that exalteth itself against*

the knowledge of God, and bringing into captivity every thought to the obedience of Christ." (2 Corinthians 10:5)

What to Do About Masturbation

Masturbation is **not** one of those acts where you promise never to do it again and stop. At least that was not the case for me. During my single years of struggles I got busy and set goals for myself. I got more into the Bible and became very active in church. Every time there was a church service, I was there. When we didn't have anything going on, I visited other churches. I began to meet other young Christians that loved God too. This gave me the motivation to keep going. I developed a relationship with my pastor and I stuck close to him. He was my covering. When I was tempted, I sought his protection by helping him with church matters. That kept me occupied. It didn't happen overnight, but I kept busy and my life became filled with the things of God.

"But put ye on the Lord Jesus Christ, and make not provision for the flesh,

> *to fulfill the lusts thereof." (Romans 13:14)*

If you are going to defeat the devil, you must learn to move ahead of him. Jesus is our perfect example of everything we will face as Christians. When Jesus was led of the Spirit to be tempted of the devil, He fasted for forty days and forty nights (Matthew 4:1-11). Jesus stayed prepared through fasting and praying. Likewise, you must discipline yourself and build a relationship with God. Start fasting and praying to God to become pure. Those who fast consistently understand that fasting is the surest way to bring the body back in line with the Spirit.

> *"For the flesh lusteth against the Spirit and the Spirit against the flesh: and these are contrary the one to the other: so that ye cannot do the things that ye would. But if ye be led of the Spirit, ye are not under the law." (Galatians 5:17-18)*

Also, remember to think on these things:

- You are a holy vessel; watch your life of association. If you are recovering from sin, it is wise to talk to someone that you can be accountable to. It is encouraging and motivating to be in the company of others who are praying, reading the bible and sharing their faith. As a team, we are strong.

  "Two are better than one; because they have a good reward of their labor." (Ecclesiastes 4:9)

  "For where two or three are gathered together in my name, there am I in the midst of them." (Matthew 18:20)

- Repent. Repent. Repent. The flesh enjoys masturbation but not your spirit. That is why you must keep repenting. Since we know that the flesh is weak, feed your spirit with spiritual things and watch what you read and hear. Even guard your spirit when the television is on. You can't watch everything and expect to resist temptation.

Watch and pray, that ye enter not into temptation: the spirit indeed is willing, but the flesh is weak." (Matthew 26:41)

"When tempted, no one should say, "God is tempting me." For God cannot be tempted by evil, nor does he tempt anyone; but each one is tempted when, by his own evil desire, he is dragged away and enticed. Then, after desire has conceived, it gives birth to sin; and sin, when it is full-grown, gives birth to death." (James 1:13-15 NIV)

Men who spend the majority of their time worrying about carnal things are basically the ones that are secretly struggling the most with human sexuality. *"If I regard iniquity in my heart, the Lord will not hear me." (Psalms 66:18)* They have shut God out of their lives and are attempting to fix things on their own. If you are dealing with a situation that is getting the best of you, find a pastor or other strong Christian who will stand with you in prayer. Overcoming masturbation is a process and you may not stop immediately, but you must continue to seek the Lord until you reach your breakthrough.

CHAPTER EIGHT

Turning Your Experience Into Ministry

When a person has survived being in jail, they have a special love for life and cherish things they once took for granted. They can be used by God to bring healing to the lives of many; however, because Satan comes to steal, kill, and destroy (John 10:10) he will try to contaminate their lives with bitterness. Satan knows that when a person is bitter, they do not want to help anybody because they feel as though they don't have anything to offer.

God has sent me to tell you that **your mess is your message!** It is through your brokenness that

God will use you to speak healing into the life of someone else. In the process you will find meaning for your own life.

Whatever you experience in life will eventually be used again. Although I have never been arrested I know the pain of incarceration from another perspective. For most of my childhood, I was held in captivity because of low self-esteem.

My pain, resulting from the bondage of insecurities, has turned into a ministry of compassion for those who are hurting. My sexual struggles have given me the experience and ability to speak openly to others about this sensitive matter. Oftentimes men seek my counsel for their sexual struggles. They immediately discern that I am approachable, therefore, they feel comfortable talking to me about whatever is on their mind. I regularly hear people say, "I have never shared this with anyone before but I know you are a man of God and for some reason I feel comfortable talking to you." Many of these people are complete strangers but they are easily drawn to me because of the anointing God has placed on my life.

When I first recognized the call of God to go into ministry, I was untrained in the things I knew that God was calling me to do. I did not like to read, I hated Sunday school, and did not like to talk in front of people. It takes all those qualities and more to become a preacher. But yet, in spite of all my insufficiencies, God was able to take what the devil meant for evil and turn it around for His purpose. I invite you to read my story and hopefully you will be encouraged that great testimonies can come out of your troublesome situation as well, provided that you put your trust in God.

My Story

I grew up in Robertsville, South Carolina, a very small town of approximately 500 people. My family was poor, however we had more than many of our neighbors and relatives.

Growing up in the South during the 1950s was difficult if you needed medical attention. My mother was always sickly and was admitted into the hospital quite frequently. I remember many holidays wishing she were at home. My mother had diabetes, but many years had gone by before it was properly diagnosed. Because doctors knew that she was under a lot of stress, they only focused on her high blood pressure. The doctors were so concerned about her blood pressure that they would often retain her in the office for a few hours thinking that she would have a stroke or a heart attack. Unfortunately, diabetes, if left unchecked, will eventually affect the mind and cause hallucination and other physical imbalance; therefore, the doctors thought my mother had a mental problem.

It was hard to accept what was happening to us. My father did the best he could to keep us together and take care of us. However, there were times when we couldn't stay home with him due to my mother's lengthy hospital stays. My father drove over 60 miles one-way to work plus he worked overtime to provide for us. Because half of us were very young he felt it was best that we were not left alone for those many hours. I am the youngest of seven children. My three older brothers stayed with one set of relatives and I stayed with another, along with my two sisters, since I was closer to them in age. My oldest sister was married and did not live with us. Yet, she and her husband made many sacrifices for us. There was a time when I didn't know my brothers as well as I knew my sisters. However, as we grew older, our sufferings brought us closer together. I am grateful for my aunts and uncles who stepped in and took care of us.

As we grew older, my mother's sickness began to take a toll on all of us, especially me.

When my mother had to make one of her frequent trips to the hospital, she would get picked up in the sheriff's car. If she were not able to sit up for the ride, the mortician used his hearse and took her. (During those days the morticians often used their hearse as an ambulance). It was embarrassing because everyone would be watching. I was humiliated because kids teased me at school. Think about what we had to go through as children. Kids don't know any better; they will tease you about everything. It was difficult to keep up with all the pressure I was under as a child. I began to fall behind in school because of low self-esteem. I felt as if I was not as good as others. I was angry and I blamed everyone, including my father, for what we were going through. I kept wishing it were a bad dream. Many years later I realized that my father was doing a lot for us and he was not the blame.

I did not like to fight so I was also a victim of kids taking advantage of me. It was affecting me in many ways. A few times I had no choice but to fight when someone tried to take my lunch money or my school supplies.

At five years old I was introduced to sex. Older kids are notorious for introducing younger kids to things they are not prepared for. I certainly wasn't ready for all that I saw and experienced as a little boy. The worst part about it is that younger kids seem to take matters further than what they learn from older kids. Many rapists and serial killers were molested or involved in some form of sexual abuse as a child and they took it to a level of crime. They started out as the victim. Today they are the victors.

I remember older boys telling me about what they had done to girls and enticing me to do the same. I also remember those little girls holding up their dresses in front of me and the boys telling me to go ahead and "do it." The first time I saw the nakedness of a girl, I ran. When the bigger boys found out, they made fun of me.

I always found myself unsupervised with older girls wanting to experiment on my body. Of course I was scared at first. (God intended for sex to be pleasurable between a man and a woman, but when it's a child, it leaves emotional scars behind. The damage usually will surface later).

By the time I became a teenager, I resented girls. I didn't trust them. In fact, I didn't trust boys either. It was also during this time my body was changing and I was having sexual struggles and didn't know where to turn. In the process of time, I went into isolation.

It doesn't take much for a teenage boy to experiment sexually, especially when he is frustrated with life. That's exactly what happened to me. I experimented with all kinds of things, which led me to pornography and other forms of perversion. The bad part about sexual perversion is, it will rob you of what is natural.

At the age of fourteen, I accepted Jesus into my heart as my personal savior. Being a Christian is a process. Everything doesn't happen over night. Little did I know that I was in for a long road of test and temptations. Through it all, I was glad to have God in my life. I began to reverence God and to seek Him to become pure.

I was at the age when a young male's, hormones really kick-in; therefore, I struggled to stay pure. Because I held so many things within, it was not long before I plunged back into pornography and many secret sins. It's not that the Holy Spirit wasn't doing its job, I was just naive. When the Spirit was trying to lead me around the pitfalls, I was too ignorant to recognize and see the big picture. I was actually fighting the Holy Spirit.

There was very little teaching in the church for young people when I was a teenager. The most an older man said to a boy was "fast and pray" if they said anything at all. The devil took the upper hand on me because of my lack of knowledge. I thought everybody in church was holy. I soon found out better. It was a struggle for me to keep going because people kept disappointing me.

I even encountered a few lustful men who tried to entice me. As time went on, I found myself avoiding people. I was caught in a difficult situation because I didn't know whom to trust and became paranoid.

Evangelist Mabel S. Butler was my pastor. We were a small family church and the majority of the members were females. There were a few guys in church with me, but they began to fall by the wayside one by one. Soon there was only one other male in the church beside myself and he eventually slacked up too. I kept going in spite of being called a pimp or gay. The women in my church were all loving Christians. Nevertheless, I was uncomfortable because of my past.

I cannot stress it enough, do not leave God if you are struggling. You may have to walk alone for a season but stay with God!

My pastor died before my eighteenth birthday. After several months without a pastor our church merged with another church and Bishop H. Manker was my new pastor, who eventually became my father-in-law. I know for sure that God is faithful to all that call upon Him. I needed a male figure in my life to help shape me into a dedicated Christian. God saw my struggles and caused our paths to cross. He took me under his mentorship and I became comfortable because he was a very decent and godly man.

> *"And the Lord said, I have surely seen the affliction of my people which are in Egypt, and have heard their cry by reason of their taskmasters; for I know their sorrows" (Exodus 3:7).*

> *"But when he saw the multitudes, he was moved with compassion on them,*

because they fainted, and were scattered abroad, as sheep having no shepherd" (Matthew 9:36).

The above scriptures are what compelled me to write about my life. I exposed myself because I want you to feel my heartbeat. I want to share and let you know that you are not alone. God cares about you. I sense an urgency to get this book into the hands of hurting people. It is my goal to help someone. If you are down, you can get up again.

I did not have all the answers back then, however, God has taught me so much because of my determination. He has set me free. Today I can walk you through the process because I have lived through what I have written about. I have been on both sides of the fence. I know what it is to be messed-up sexually with all kinds of unmentionable thoughts running through my mind. And, as an ordained minister, I have a healthy marriage and a good thought pattern with the help of God. I am not above temptation but I have learned from my failures by studying my habits and daily routines. I know how to guard my spirit because the devil comes periodically to see what I am doing. I am transparent for those who need someone to relate to them. Do not live in denial. We are at war with our flesh!

Many of us are victims of circumstances. Life has dealt all of us some misfortunes. If you are empty because of what has happened to you, you need a dose of self-esteem and you need to know who you are and to whom you belong. You are God's servant. Stop wasting time worrying about the past and how you are hurting. Work on putting on more of God. He will give you the strength to deal with anything.

You may not necessarily go into prison ministry but the things you have suffered will help you to recognize your assignment and enable you to find out what God wants you to do.

May God take your mess and turn it into your message.

CHAPTER 9

Free At Last

"And he shall be like a tree planted by the rivers of water, that bringeth forth his fruit in his season; his leaf also shall not wither; and whatsoever he doeth shall prosper." (Psalms 1:3)

It is time to do something with your life. In order for your dreams to come true you must get started. Opportunity is available regardless of what has happened to you. You can determine your destiny by your attitude and your actions. As you recall from my personal story, I was set free because of my determination. No matter how far you have fallen, determination will cause you to see the light. Determination will move you to follow God's will rather than your own feelings. You must do what you don't feel like doing until your flesh gets out of the way. If you don't have the energy to do what you know you need to do, it is because you are not as close to God as you need to be.

Closeness is how you will get the strength to resist the devil. Keep in mind the battle is not yours. It belongs to God. God is the one that fights for us. It is your job to stay pure in the sight of God. You do this by constantly confessing your sins every time you do wrong and asking God to take sin away from you.

So as you can see, there is a sequence to freedom. First you must submit to God. As you draw near to God, He will draw near to you.

> *"Submit yourselves therefore to God. Resist the devil, and he will flee from you." (James 4:8)*

Then you must confess your sins. Confession is two-fold — It releases the power of God, which sets you free; and it also defeats the devil and kicks him out of the driver's seat.

> *"He that covereth his sins shall not prosper: but whoso confesseth and forsaketh them shall have mercy."* (Proverbs 28:13)

We are accustomed to the saying, "talk is cheap." The real truth of the matter is talk is expensive because what you confess out of your mouth can cost your life. If you are determined to walk closer with God and be set free from sin, start by confessing the following:

- I am a child of God.
- I am a new person in Christ Jesus; the old is gone and the new has come.
- I am chosen for God's special use.
- I am precious in the sight of God.
- I am a royal priesthood.
- I am free from shame because of the blood of Jesus.

The more you repeat who you are, it will affect the way you think. God will honor your confessions and you will see Him at work in your life.

You should also begin to confess what you want to do. The more you repeat your desires before God, eventually things will unfold and you will begin to sense on the inside what God will have you to do. Remember, it all starts with rehearsing to God what you are going to do. Every morning you should open your mouth and repeat your desires to God. It may seem like something small but don't underestimate what God will do. There are creative abilities within you that you need to command to come alive. Speak it out of your mouth until your thinking changes. Speak it until you get your confidence back. Speak it until you re-connect with your destiny. The ultimate blessing is not material things but it is the peace of God in your heart.

> *And let the peace of God rule in your hearts, to which also ye are called in one body; and be ye thankful. (Colossians 3:15)*

For those that have many years behind bars, you also have the potential to become active for God by helping others find their way to God. I have met many inmates who got saved while incarcerated that God is now using to share the good news of Jesus Christ with their fellow inmates. One young man stated that God placed him in jail to save his life. Five of his buddies have died since his arrest; four of them were killed on the streets, and one committed suicide. He said that if he were not in jail today, he probably would be dead. He is being used by God to deliver the gospel, and many lives are being drawn to God because of the radiant light that is shining through him.

I met another young man, who declared that it took having his back against the wall for God to get his attention. He is amazed at the anointing and power of God that is drawing other men to the Christian faith. He says that he is grateful for a second chance but feels unworthy to have others looking to him for direction.

When you decide to surrender to the will of God, He will do the rest. You will not have to do anything out of the ordinary to promote yourself.

*"A man's gift maketh room for him,
and bringeth him before great men."
(Proverbs 18:16)*

Understanding the Anointing

You must understand that the anointing is a gift. It is not something that you work for, although you will learn that you must use self-control to maintain it. (For example, the Bible character Samson had lots of energy but lacked the wisdom it took to maintain his anointing.) The anointing is the God given ability that comes upon a person to carry out a special assignment. However, there are levels of anointing based upon the assignment. Once you become a Christian you have been anointed. Everyone has three basic gifts whether they are a preacher or not. These gifts will cause you to start operating in the anointing. They are the gift of faith, the gift of healing, and the gift of salvation. First of all, we have the ability to believe which is the gift of faith. Along with that we have the ability to cause others to believe too. Secondly, we have the ability to be healed both emotionally and physically by the power of God. We also have the ability to cause someone else to receive healing by sharing our experience and convincing him or her to believe for the same. Thirdly, we have the ability to receive salvation for our lives, and then we have the ability to persuade others to become a Christian by sharing the good news of the gospel with them.

By now, you probably realize that my gift is salvation and God has anointed me to use this gift in prison ministry. Let me share one last testimony with you.

Some time ago, I went to court with a friend whose son was on trial for a crime. She feared the worse and asked me to go with her as a means of support. I arrived at the courthouse early that morning and sat through many cases, which broke my heart. As I quietly sat in my seat I watched dozens of guys being sent to prison. Her son was the last one to go before the judge and the only one who was released that day. I thought for sure I would see him in church after that, but needless to say he kept going in the wrong direction. I did not hear from him until he got arrested again. Although I very was disappointed in him, I knew I had to do something. From that experience I was inspired to get involved with prison ministry. I sensed in my spirit a strong desire to talk to as many inmates as possible in an attempt to give them some guidelines for survival after jail.

Pay attention to what upsets or disappoints you

because typically it is linked to your desires, and this could indicate an opportunity where, in due season, God wants to prosper you.

    I pray that from reading this book, you are able to get beyond the surface and experience the peace and freedom that only God can give you — not the world. Regardless of your situation, your future is in God's hand. He has not turned His back on you no matter how dark it may seem. This is not the end of the road for you. It is time to watch your mistakes turn into miracles through the power of God. Use your energy in a positive way because God can work through you behind bars. No matter what has bound your life, in the name of our Lord Jesus Christ, you can be free at last!

Conclusion

You have covered a series of practical and workable techniques for living a successful Christian life behind bars as well as when you are released.

The biblical stories and case studies of inmates were used as examples to demonstrate that through godly wisdom and knowledge you, too, can receive similar results. Please know that reading is not enough. Keep studying until you obtain the desired results.

We may never meet in person, but in this book we have cried, prayed and studied together. We are closer than you think. It will give me great pleasure

Do You Have A Loved One In Jail?

to know that this book has made a difference in your life. Feel free to write me with your testimony or prayer request at:

    Dr. Marvin Scott, Ph.D.
    Outreach Deliverance Ctr
    P. O. Box 150012
    Alexandria, VA 22315

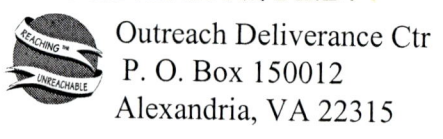

May God help you to walk with Him and bless your life with success.

Printed in the United States
23264LVS00002B/160-408